MIND BOGGLERS

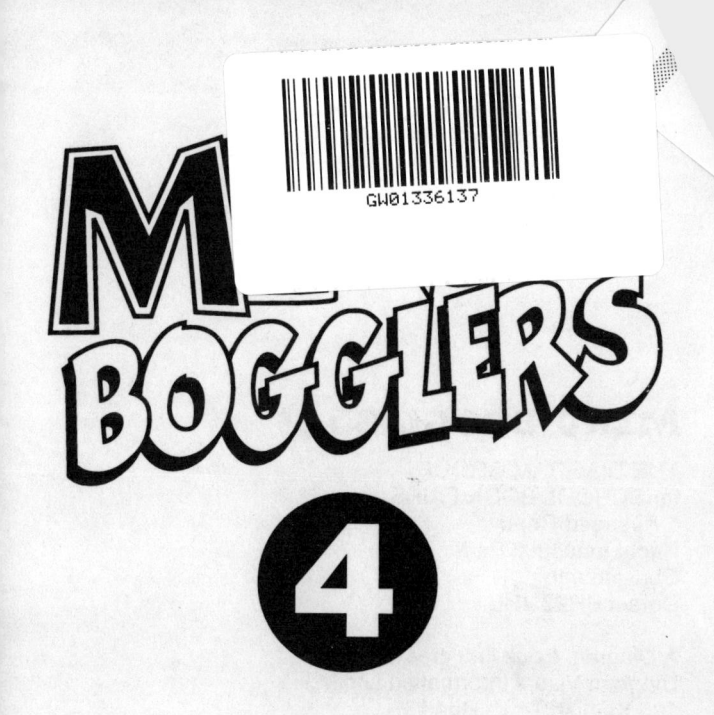

4

THE DIAGRAM GROUP

MIND BOGGLERS 4

THE DIAGRAM GROUP
for SCHOOL BOOK FAIRS
5 Airspeed Road
Priory Industrial Park
Christchurch
Dorset BH23 4HD

A Diagram Book first created by
Diagram Visual Information Limited
195 Kentish Town Road
London NW5 8SY

First published 1995

Reprint 10 9 8 7 6 5 4 3 2 1 0

© Diagram Visual Information Limited 1995

ISBN 1-900121-03-4
All rights reserved

Printed in Great Britain

Namesake
These two animals have almost the same name. A zebra lives in Africa and a zubra lives in Poland and Russia.

Not a part of a bird
A dovetail is a way of joining two pieces of wood. Their ends are cut into special interlocking shapes.

Seasick seaman
Horatio Lord Nelson was one of Britain's greatest admirals. But he was often seasick for the first few days of a voyage.

Leaping lions

Lions are shown on badges, coins, flags and stamps. There is a special name for each way a lion leaps, stands, sits or lies.

1 Lion rampant
2 Lion statant
3 Lion rampant guardant
4 Lion passant
5 Lion statant
6 Lion passant guardant
7 Lion sejant
8 Lion sejant rampant
9 Lion couchant
10 Lion salient
11 Lion coward
12 Lion queue fourchée

So many cells

The back of your eye is called the retina. Although it is quite small, it contains 137 million cells. It has 130 million cells to help you see black and white, and seven million cells to help you see colours.

This is the actual size of your retina.

Mini molecules

A molecule is a tiny piece of something, so small you can only see one with a powerful microscope. Molecules are so tiny that one spoon of water contains as many of them as there are spoons of water in the Atlantic.

Typecast
Over 100 years ago, some scientists believed that the shape of your head showed the type of personality you had. Are any of your friends' heads shaped like one of these?

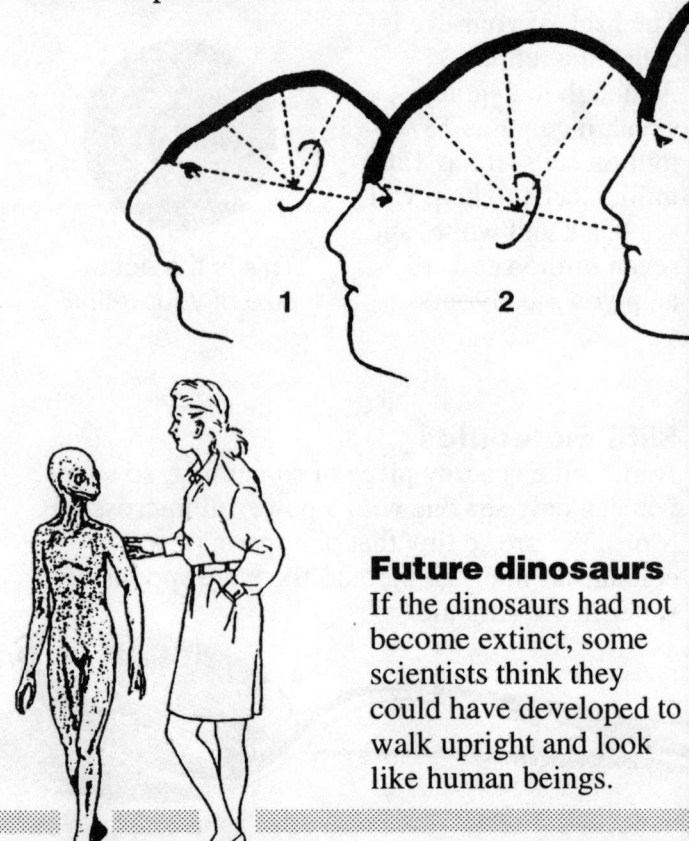

Future dinosaurs
If the dinosaurs had not become extinct, some scientists think they could have developed to walk upright and look like human beings.

1 Idiot
2 Criminal
3 Poet or thinker
4 Likely to commit crimes
5 Likely to be honest

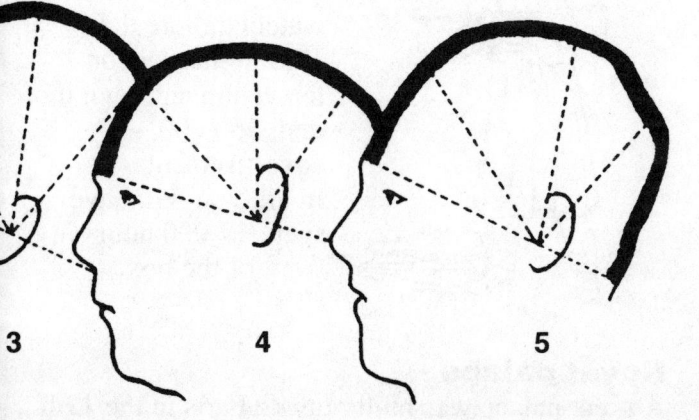

3   **4**   **5**

Startling eyes

When this moth has its wings folded, it looks like a piece of old bark. If a bird comes near, it opens its wings and shows two spots that look like eyes. The startled bird is likely to fly off without trying to peck at the moth.

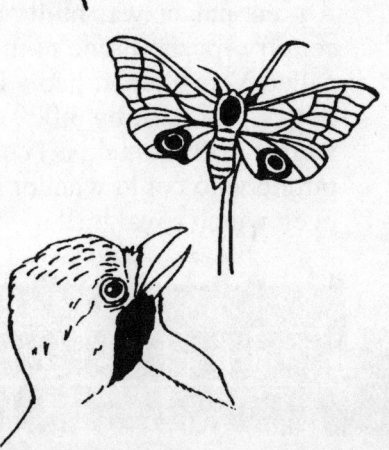

Box gogglers

It is estimated that by the time you are 18 years old, you will have watched more than 15,000 murders on television and seen more than 360,000 advertisements.
In all, you will have spent 17,000 hours in front of the box.

Royal palace

A great palace was built outside Paris in the 17th century for the French king, Louis XIV. It was called Versailles. It had a Hall of Mirrors 73 metres (240 ft) long, lit by 3,000 candles. In the gardens were 1,400 fountains. The palace was open to the public who could wander through its rooms and even watch royal births.

What a corker!

Table tennis was invented by James Gibb over 100 years ago. It was first played with bats made from cigar-box lids and champagne corks for balls. The game is also called ping pong.

Walking on water

A South American lizard can walk on water, but not for very long. It has powerful back legs and broad feet with fringed toes that keep it afloat. When scared by a predator, the lizard leaps from the river bank and dashes across the water for as long as it can. Once it sinks, it can stay underwater for up to two minutes.

Whose side are you on?
The pages of this book each have two sides. Turn over and look at the back of this one. You can make a strip of paper that has only one side. You don't believe it? Take a strip of paper. Twist it once and glue the ends together. Now try to colour only one side of the whole strip.

Pedal power
A bicycle, ridden by three men and mounted on canoes, travelled down the River Thames from Oxford to London faster than an ordinary boat rowed by three men.

Outnumbered
There are over 4,000 different types of mammal, including human beings. But there are over 23,000 different types of fish.

Friendly foe
Only gorillas in zoos eat meat. Those in the wild, which are free, eat only fruit and vegetables.

Sinking city

Mexico City is built on an underground reservoir. Each year, the number of people in the city grows and more water is taken out of the reservoir. As a result, the city is slowly sinking at a rate of about 15–20 cm (6–8 in) a year. This picture shows the city in the middle of a lake at the time when Europeans first explored America.

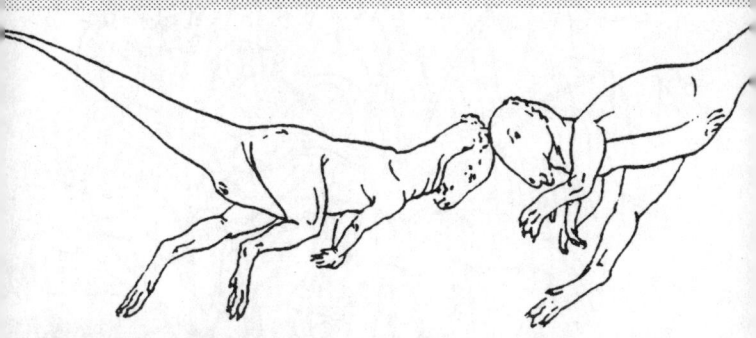

Head-bangers

Some dinosaurs fought for food or for females by charging at each other and banging heads. Called 'boneheads', they had thick skulls to protect their brains.

Sowing seeds

This bracket fungus, a type of mushroom, sheds its seeds, called spores, at a rate of 30,000 million a day for six months.

Talking trees

Scientists have discovered that trees may be able to talk to each other using a chemical language. When one tree is attacked by caterpillars which feed on its leaves, it sends out chemical signals to other trees. The trees' leaves make substances that the pests dislike and this prevents the caterpillars from spreading to the other trees and eating them alive.

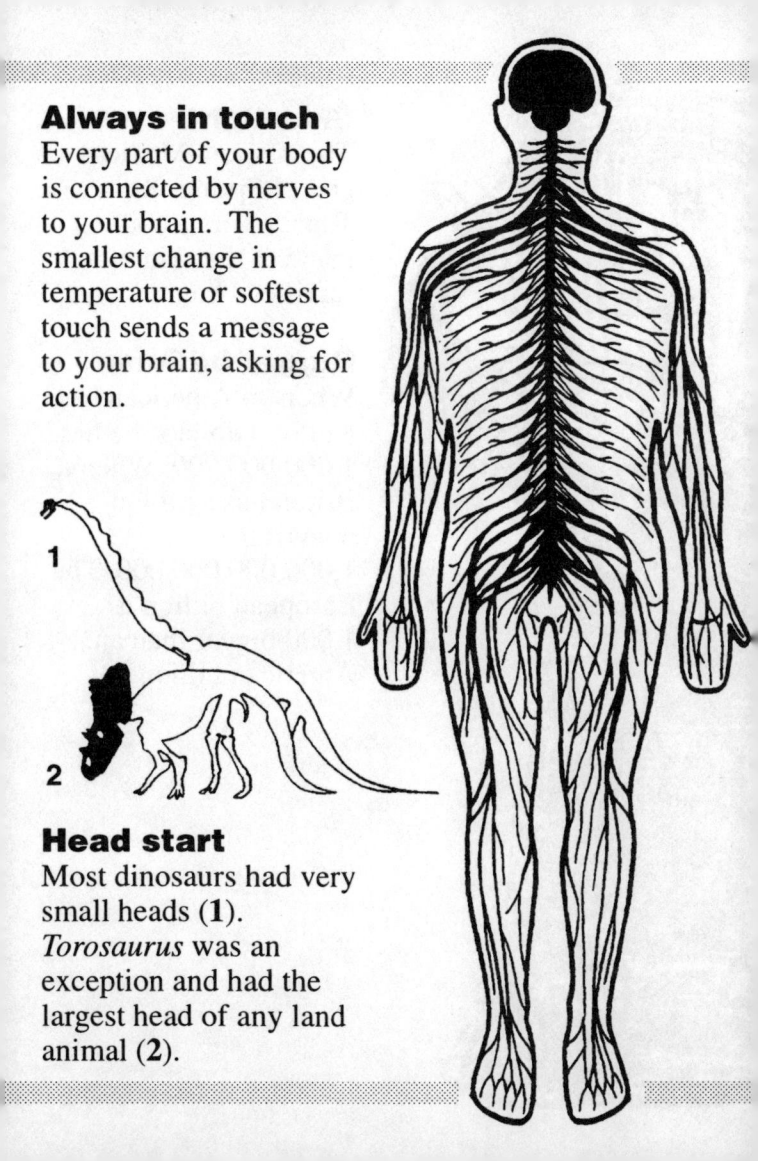

Always in touch
Every part of your body is connected by nerves to your brain. The smallest change in temperature or softest touch sends a message to your brain, asking for action.

Head start
Most dinosaurs had very small heads (**1**). *Torosaurus* was an exception and had the largest head of any land animal (**2**).

Skin tight

The Ancient Mexican god of Spring, Xipe Topec, wore a coat made of the skin of a sacrificed human.

Bigger billions

When an American has a billion dollars, he has 1,000,000,000. When a Briton has a billion pounds, he has 1,000,000,000,000. The European billion is 1,000 bigger than an American billion.

On its back
This tiny shrimp, called a brine shrimp, swims along upside down, moving its tiny legs like the oars of a rowing boat.

Lengthy lungs
Did you know that your lungs contain a mesh of very small blood vessels called capillaries? If you laid them out end to end they would stretch for 2,400 km (1,500 miles).

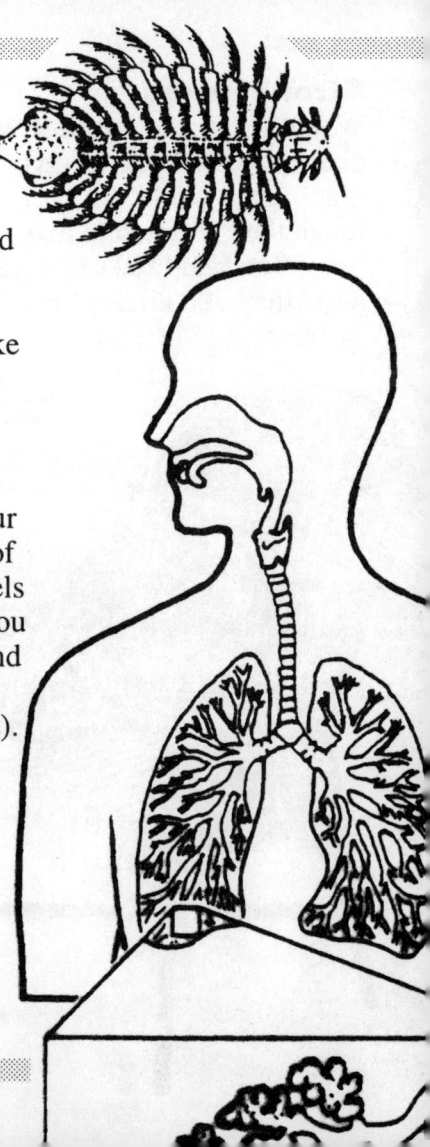

Strong grass

Would you make furniture with grass? Some people do. Bamboo is a type of grass, the largest grass in the world. Its hard, woody stems are so tough they are used to make houses, chairs, tables, beds, flutes and stakes for garden plants. There are more than 700 kinds of bamboo. Some grow up to 37 metres (122 ft) tall.

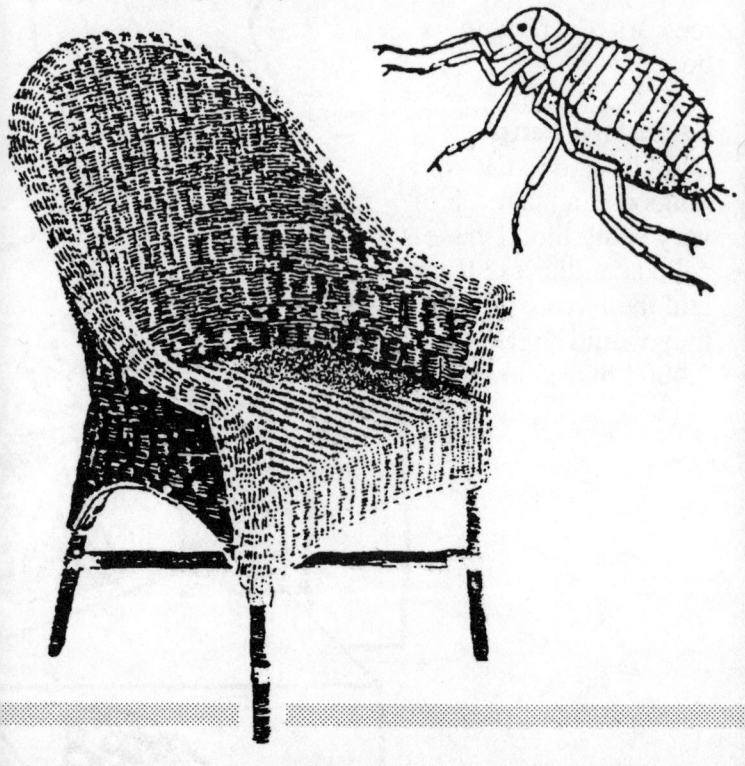

Giant pearl
One of the largest pearls, the Pearl of Laotze, was found inside a giant clam. It was 24 cm (9.5 in) long and weighed as much as a three-month-old baby.

Killer fleas
A deadly disease, called the bubonic plague, killed more than a quarter of all the people in Europe in the 14th century. The disease was spread from rats to human beings by tiny biting fleas.

Guard dog
In Ancient Greek mythology, the gates of the underworld were guarded by a dog with three heads, called Cerberus. It allowed only spirits of the dead to go in and let none out.

Colourful warning
The male anole displays his colourful throat flap to attract a female and warn off other males in the mating season. It is a member of the chameleon family.

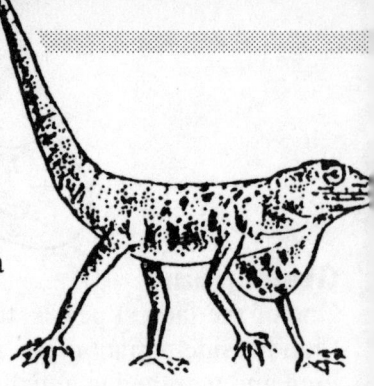

Milestones
The current record for running 1 mile (1,609 metres) is 3 min, 44.39 sec. It was set by an Algerian, Noureddine Morceli, in 1993. Until 1954, it was thought impossible that anyone could run a mile in under 4 minutes. In that year, an English medical student, Roger Bannister, ran it in 3 min, 59.4 sec.

Single parents
Male and female jaguars live apart all the year and only meet during the mating season. The female gives birth to 2–4 young and brings them up on her own.

Old paper
The oldest surviving writing paper dates back to about AD 110 and was made in China.

Superstition

Alberto Ascari won 20 Grand Prix races. He was so superstitious that he always drove wearing a lucky blue helmet and shirt. In 1955, he tried out a sports car without them and was killed.

Read all about it!

The first newspaper was printed in China about 1,300 years ago. It was called *Tching pao* – 'News of the Capital'. Another early government newspaper called *Acta Diurna* – 'Daily Happenings' – was handed out free in Ancient Rome.

Castle on a volcano

Edinburgh Castle in Scotland was built nearly 1,000 years ago on top of an old volcano. But there is no need to worry. The volcano, and another one nearby called Arthur's Seat, became extinct about 300 million years ago.

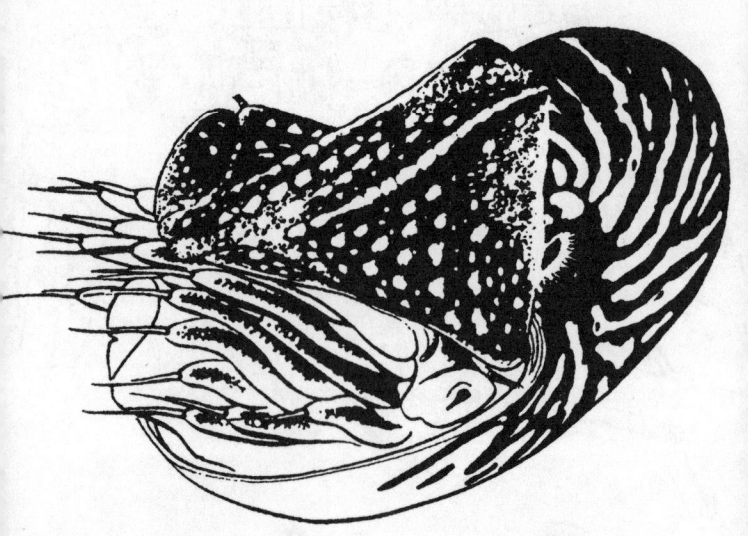

Moving house
A shellfish called a nautilus lives in a compartment in a coiled shell. As it grows, it moves out of the old compartment and builds a bigger one in front of it.

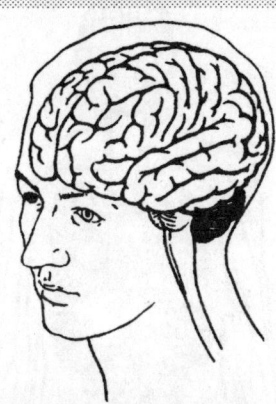

Wacky weights

An adult's brain weighs 3 lbs, which is equal to the weight of three soccer balls.

Exploding balls

During the Second World War, the Germans dropped iron balls full of explosives (mines) into the sea. When a passing ship bumped into the floating ball and touched the points, the bomb exploded.

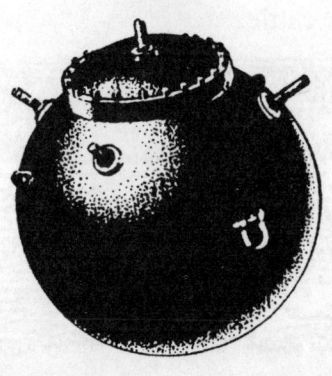

Getting about

An English doctor, William Harvey, was the first to discover, over 300 years ago, that your blood moves around your body. The blood in your big toe today may be in your ear tomorrow.

Not a home

Two-storey stone houses built in the English Lake District were not for people. They were winter shelters for cattle.

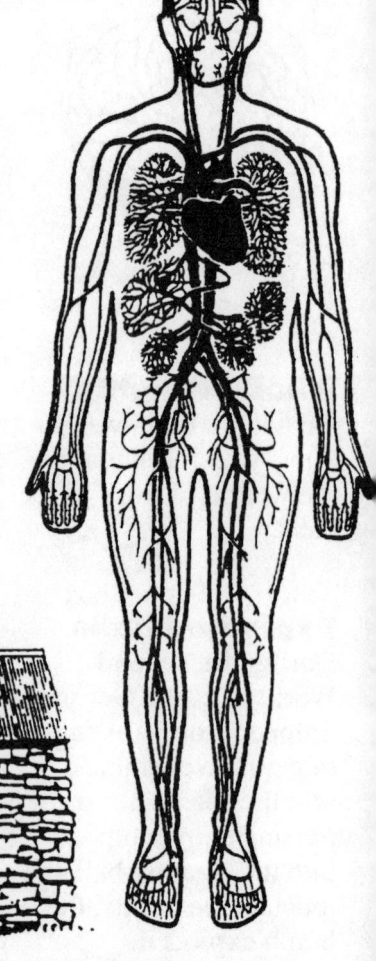

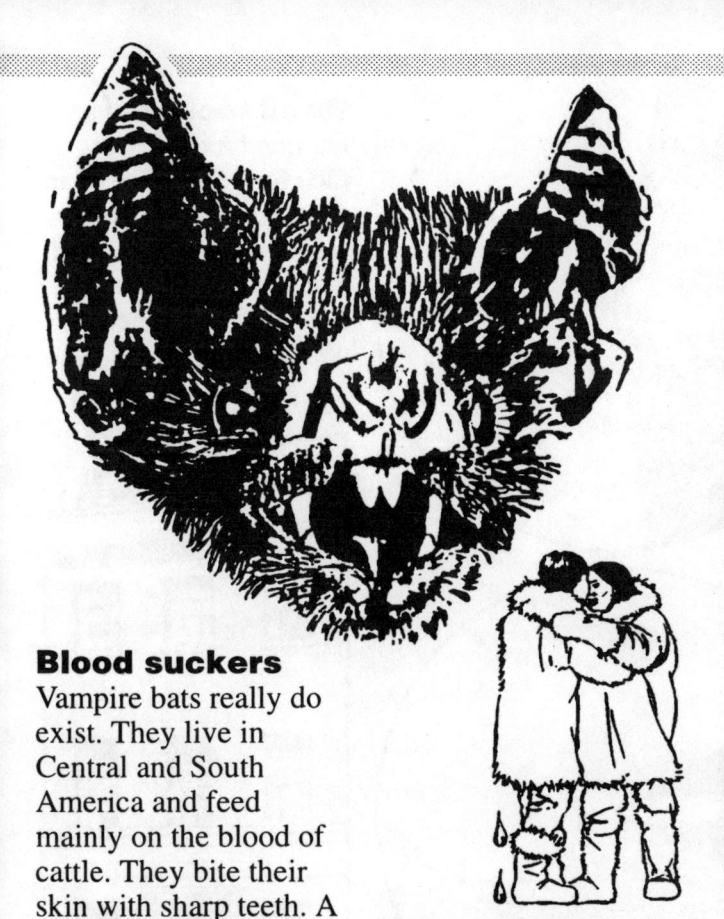

Blood suckers
Vampire bats really do exist. They live in Central and South America and feed mainly on the blood of cattle. They bite their skin with sharp teeth. A special substance in their saliva stops the blood from clotting while they lap it up.

Nose greeting
Eskimos say hello, goodbye and kiss by rubbing noses.

Good looker
Human beings' eyes face forwards. They can see ahead and to each side. Fish, with eyes on the sides of their heads, can see behind them as well as in front.

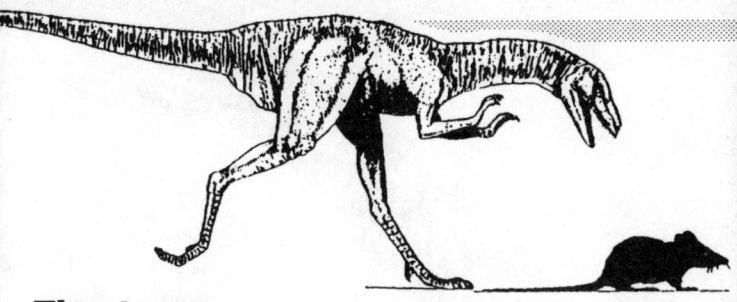

Tiny terror

Not all dinosaurs were huge monsters. This one, which lived about 150 million years ago, was only the size of a cat.

Back to front

No. 10 Downing Street, the official home of the British Prime Minister, is back to front. The famous front door is really the back entrance to two houses which are now joined into one.

'Mysterious dogs'

American Indians caught and rode horses first brought to North America by Europeans. The Indians called them 'mysterious dogs'.

Pet monster
The Hellbender is a giant salamander, about 76 cm (30 in) long. When kept as a pet, it will eat dog food.

Growth check
A baby grows fastest in the last three months before it is born. If it continued to grow at that rate it would be 5.5 metres (18 ft 4 in) tall by 10 years of age.

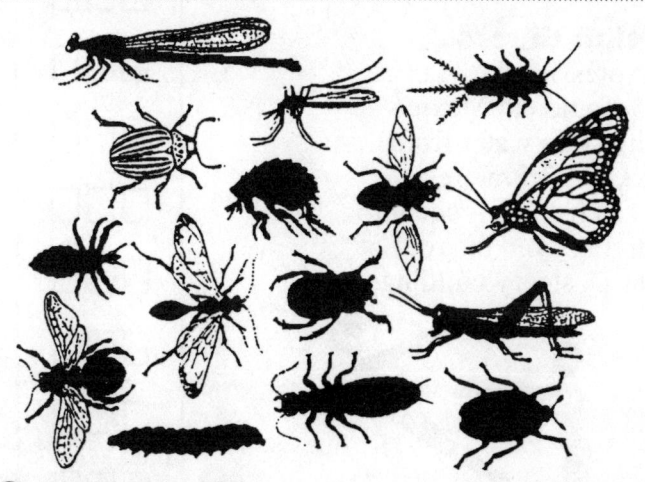

Creepy-crawly
Of all the different species of animal on Earth, nearly half of them are insects – there are over 950,000 different kinds.

Satchmo
Louis Armstrong, the great American jazz musician, learned to play the trumpet while he was in an orphans' home in New Orleans.

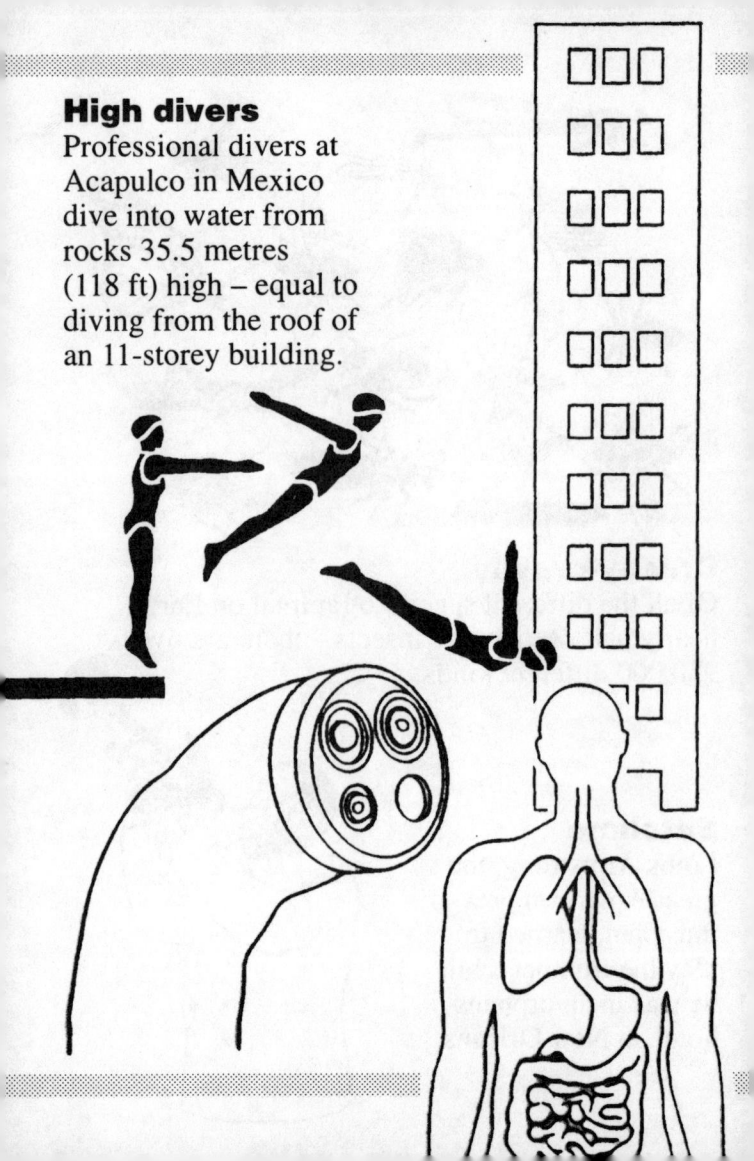

High divers
Professional divers at Acapulco in Mexico dive into water from rocks 35.5 metres (118 ft) high – equal to diving from the roof of an 11-storey building.

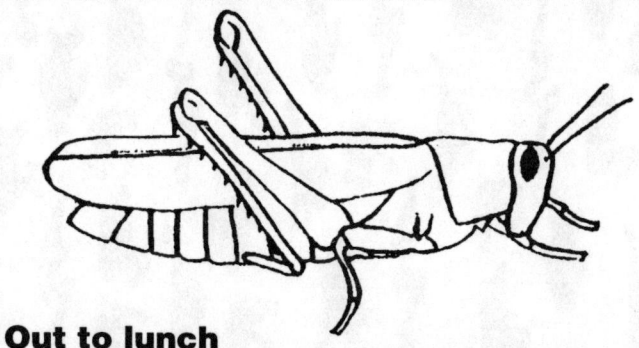

Out to lunch
A swarm of North African locusts can be so big it forms a black cloud which blocks out the sun. A single swarm may have over 50,000 million locusts in it and cover 1,000 sq km (400 sq miles). A swarm feeds at dawn and dusk, eating 3,000 tonnes of plants every day.

Inside view
Doctors can now look inside your body without having to cut you open. They put in a very thin fibre-optic tube. At the end of the tube is a light and a tiny camera. It sends back pictures so the doctors can see what is wrong with you and if you need surgery.

From out of the sky
There have been many reports of animals and fish falling out of the sky. No one knows how they get up there, although some people think they are swept up by strong winds. Here are some examples.

1 Bergen, Norway, 1578. Yellow mice fell into the sea and then swam ashore.
2 Singapore, 1861. After an earthquake, fish fell on the streets and bucketfuls were picked up.
3 Memphis, USA, 1877. Thousands of snakes dropped out of the sky during a rain storm.
4 Birmingham, Britain, 1954. Hundreds of frogs fell on people's heads and hopped around in the streets.
5 Maryland, USA, 1969. Hundreds of dead ducks dropped down on to the streets.

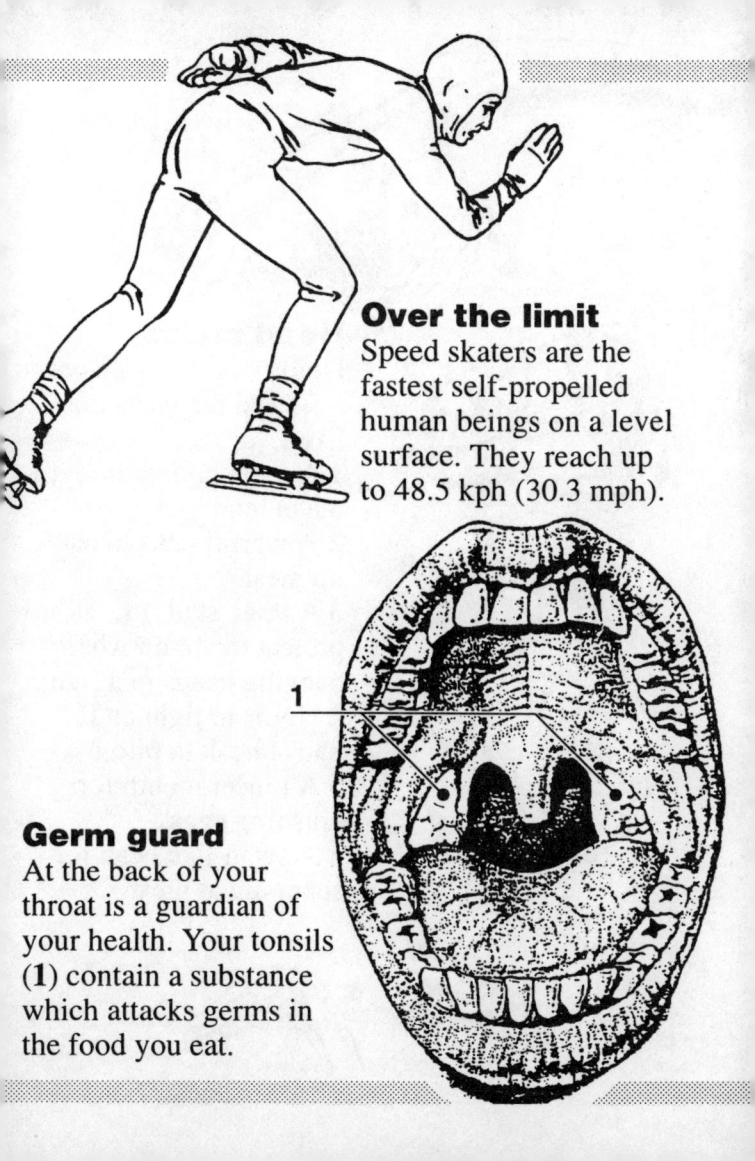

Over the limit
Speed skaters are the fastest self-propelled human beings on a level surface. They reach up to 48.5 kph (30.3 mph).

Germ guard
At the back of your throat is a guardian of your health. Your tonsils (**1**) contain a substance which attacks germs in the food you eat.

Head styles

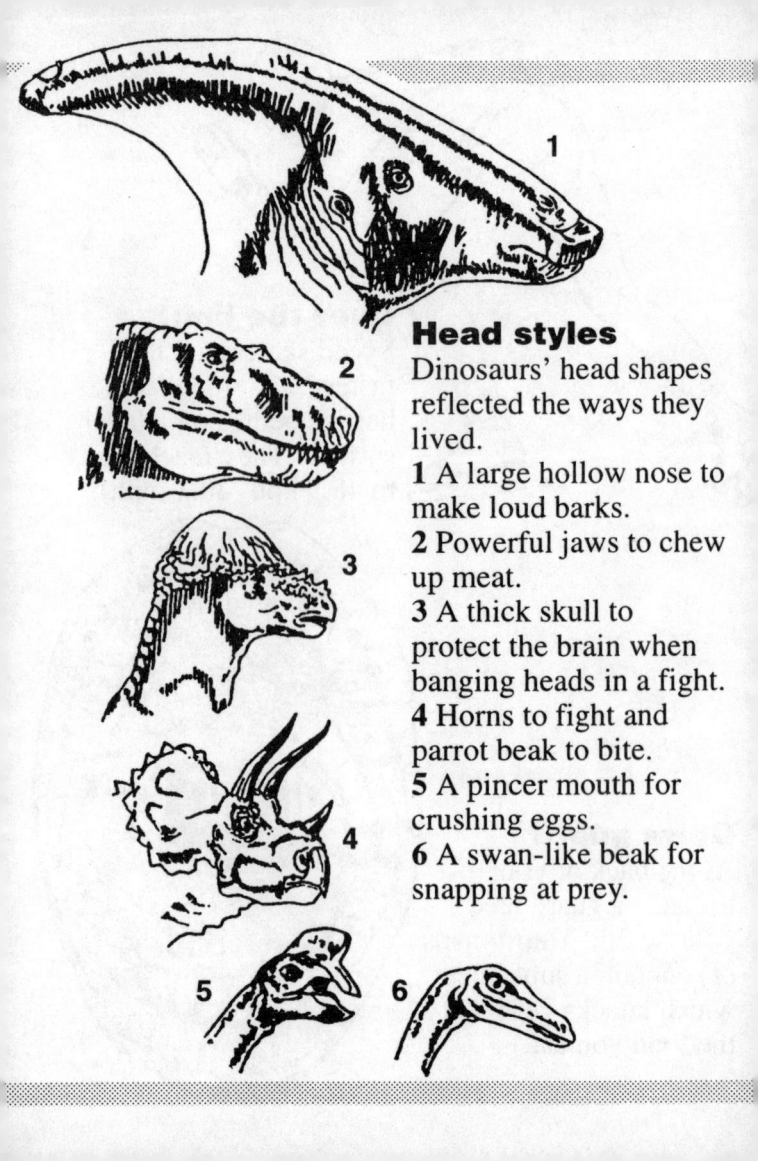

Dinosaurs' head shapes reflected the ways they lived.
1 A large hollow nose to make loud barks.
2 Powerful jaws to chew up meat.
3 A thick skull to protect the brain when banging heads in a fight.
4 Horns to fight and parrot beak to bite.
5 A pincer mouth for crushing eggs.
6 A swan-like beak for snapping at prey.

Inside story
There are worms which live in animal and even human intestines. Some are tiny but a tapeworm can grow up to 9 metres (30 ft) long.

Feather talk
American Plains Indians wore feathers in their hair as a mark of victory over the enemy. The position of a feather and the paint on it carried messages, like these:
1 I was the third to wound the enemy in battle.
2 I killed three.
3 I cut his throat and scalped him.
4 I was wounded in battle.

Getting the hump
There are two types of camel. A dromedary has one hump with a back like a D on its side. A Bactrian camel has two humps with a back like a B on its side.

Meatless monster
Adolf Hitler, the leader of the Germans during the 1930s and the Second World War, is said to have never eaten meat.

Sign of the times
The Chinese used a shadow clock to tell the time over 4,500 years ago.

Fastest ever

Astronauts returning from the Moon in command module Apollo 10 in 1969 reached a speed of 39,896 kph (24,791 mph).

Fossil clues

Fossilized evidence of dinosaurs include:
1 footprint, **2** droppings, **3** print of skin, **4** eggs.

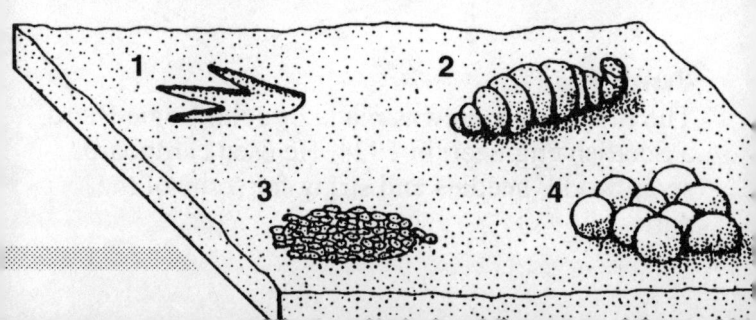

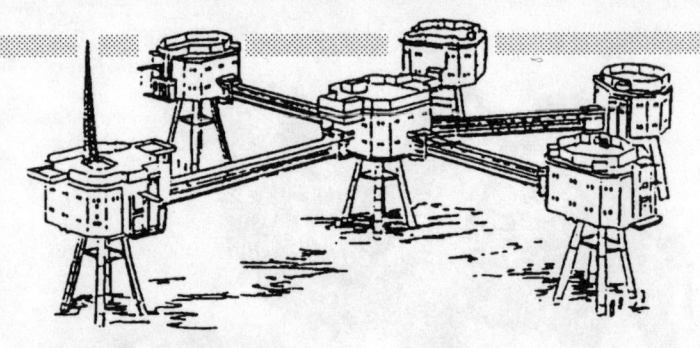

Moon station?
These castles on legs were built in Britain 50 years ago. Standing at the mouth of the River Thames, they guarded London from attack from the sea.

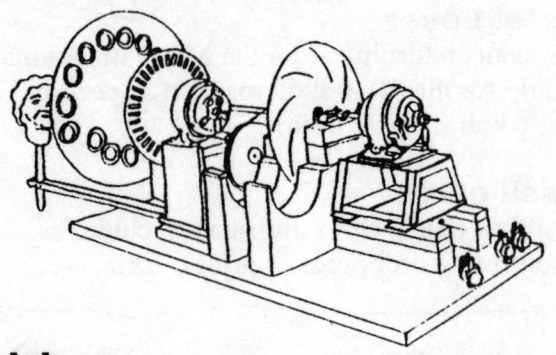

Junk box
The first television was made by John Logie Baird, a Scottish engineer, in 1924. He used cardboard, scrap wood, needles and string for some of the parts.

Super sun

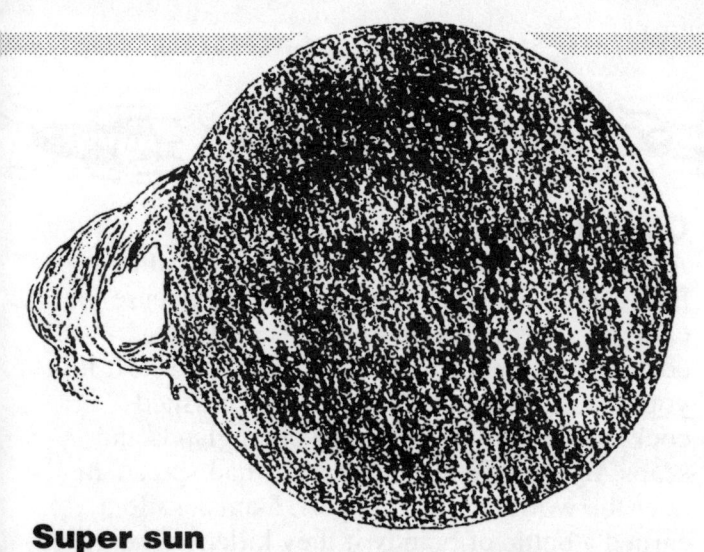

Did you know that the Sun is 150 million km (93 million miles) from the Earth? If you drove a car at 88 kph (55 mph), you would take 193 years to reach it. It is a ball of gas with a surface temperature of 2 million °C. Fountains of burning helium and hydrogen gas, called solar flares, shoot out from it into space.

Keeping warm

When you are asleep your body produces as much heat as a 100-watt light bulb.

Cockroach cure

About 2,000 years ago, a Greek doctor called Dioscorides Pedanius, believed he had a cure for earache. All you had to do was scoop out a cockroach's stomach, mix it with oil and stuff it in your ear. Later, another doctor said crushed cockroaches cured itching, swollen glands and scabs. By the 1500s, cockroaches had spread all over the world and were a pest. Danish sailors earned a bottle of brandy if they killed 1,000 of them.

Guns into medals

Britain's highest military decoration for bravery is the Victoria Cross. Queen Victoria first awarded it in 1856, at the end of the Crimean War. For many years the crosses were made of bronze from Russian guns captured during the war.

Long story
Did you know that part of your food-processing system is a long tube called the small intestine, which is coiled up inside you? If you stretched it out, it would be 6.7 metres (22 ft) long. If you opened up all the tiny wrinkles in it, it would measure 300 sq metres (360 sq yd).

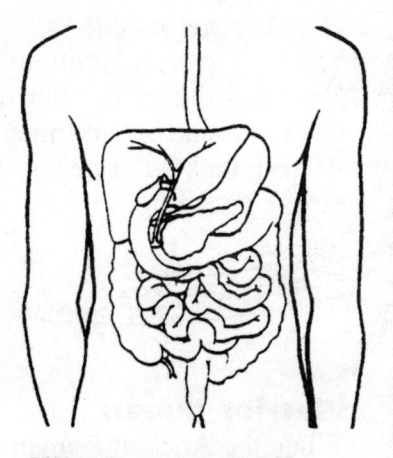

Whole new ball game
One of the world's most popular sports, so the story goes, was started by a British schoolboy. At Rugby School in 1823, William Webb Ellis was playing in a soccer match when he picked up the ball and ran with it. This was illegal but it led to the start of a new ball game – rugby football.

Neck and neck
The longest neck of all, over 14 metres (49 ft) long, was that of the dinosaur *Mamenchisaurus*. Over two-and-a-half times the height of a giraffe, its neck had the same number of bones as a giraffe's neck.

Warrior queen
When the Ancient Romans occupied Britain, Boudicca, the queen of an eastern tribe rebelled. Her army attacked Roman towns and killed over 70,000 men, woman and children.

Cell-by date

The human body has about 10 million million cells. About 3,000 million die every day and are replaced by new ones. The cells in your intestines last about three days, those in your liver about 18 months. Only the cells in your brain are never replaced.

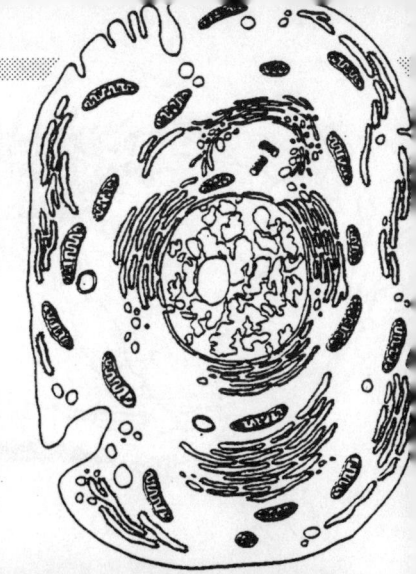

Light years away

Astronomers use the term light years to describe distances in space. There is a distant galaxy called 3C-295 which is 500 million light years away. What this really means is that it is 26,000,000,000,000,000,000,000 miles away from Earth!

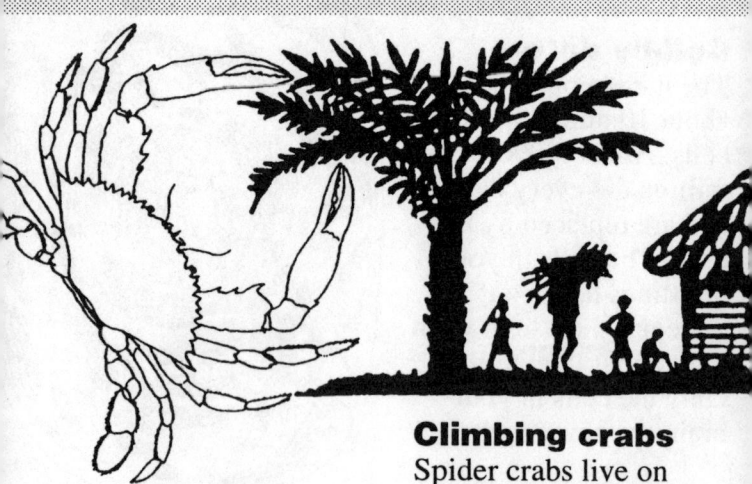

Climbing crabs
Spider crabs live on islands in the Pacific and Indian Oceans. They grow to about 45 cm (18 in) long and have very long legs, which they use to climb trees. When a crab gets to the top of a tree, it snips off a young coconut with its huge pincers and climbs down again to eat it.

Eye shadow
Ancient Egyptian women painted black eye make-up around their eyes. This helped to reduce the glare of the Sun.

Giant midgets
This is the actual size of an ant. Those in hot, wet areas of the world can be over 2.5 cm (1 in) long.

Uncle Oscar
Every year, the Academy of Motion Picture Arts and Sciences awards a trophy to people who have made an outstanding contribution to cinema. The trophy – a golden statue – used to be called The Statuette. In 1931, Margaret Herrick spotted a copy of it and said, 'Why, he looks just like my uncle Oscar.' Since then the awards ceremony and the statuettes have been called Oscars.

DID YOU KNOW?

MIND BOGGLERS 1

ONE FROG CONTAINS ENOUGH POISON TO KILL 2,200 PEOPLE ● THE MOON IS A QUARTER OF THE EARTH'S SIZE ● EARLY SPANIARDS CLEANED THEIR TEETH WITH URINE ● A BABY KANGAROO IS CALLED A JOEY

MIND BOGGLERS 2

A SIX-MONTH-OLD BABY IS AS HEAVY AS A TENPIN BOWLING BALL ● A HONEY BEE HAS FIVE EYES ● FLAT WORMS DON'T HAVE BABIES – THEY SIMPLY DIVIDE THEMSELVES INTO TWO ● ONE DINOSAUR'S LEG BONE IS TALLER THAN A MAN

MIND BOGGLERS 3

AIR-FILLED BICYCLE TYRES WERE INVENTED TWICE ● ANTS KEEP TINY CREATURES WHICH THEY MILK LIKE COWS ● SHARKS DON'T HAVE BONES IN THEIR BODIES – THEY HAVE TOUGH, FLEXIBLE CARTILAGE ● NAPOLEON PLANNED TO BUILD A CHANNEL TUNNEL NEARLY 200 YEARS AGO

IF NOT, READ THE OTHER MIND BOGGLERS!